Southern Living

Incredible Chocolate

RECIPES

Southern Living

Incredible Chocolate

RECIPES

Oxmoor House®

Southern Living® Incredible Chocolate Recipes

©2008 by Oxmoor House, Inc., Book Division of Southern Progress Corporation

P.O. Box 2262, Birmingham, Alabama 35201-2262

ISBN-13: 978-0-8487-2987-5
ISBN-10: 0-8487-2987-0
Printed in the United States of America
Second Printing 2009

Oxmoor House, Inc.
Editor in Chief: Nancy Fitzpatrick Wyatt
Executive Editor: Susan Payne Dobbs
Managing Editor: Allison Long Lowery

Southern Living® Incredible Chocolate Recipes

Editor:	Susan Hernandez Ray
Project Editor:	Vanessa Rusch Thomas
Senior Designer:	Emily Albright Parrish
Copy Chief:	L. Amanda Owens
Editorial Assistant:	Rachel Quinlivan, R.D.
Photography Director:	Jim Bathie
Senior Photographers:	Ralph Anderson, Brit Huckabay
Senior Photo Stylist:	Kay E. Clarke
Photo Stylists:	Katherine Eckert Coyne, Buffy Hargett
Test Kitchens Director:	Elizabeth Tyler Austin
Assistant Test Kitchens Director:	Julie Christopher
Test Kitchens Professionals:	Jane Chambliss; Patricia Michaud; Kathleen Royal Phillips; Catherine Crowell Steele; Ashley T. Strickland; Kate Wheeler, R.D.
Director of Production:	Laura Lockhart
Senior Production Manager:	Greg Amason
Production Manager:	Tamara Nall

Contributors

Designer:	Carol Damsky
Copy Editor:	Donna Baldone
Photographers:	Tina Cornett, William Dickey, Beau Gustafson
Photo Stylist:	Melanie Clarke
Food Stylist:	Kelley Self Wilton
Editorial Interns:	Jill Baughman, Amelia Heying, Anne-Harris Jones, Shea Staskowski
Indexer:	Mary Ann Laurens
Test Kitchens Professional:	Ana Price Kelly

Special thanks to *Southern Living*: Scott Jones, Executive Editor; Shannon Sliter Satterwhite, Food Editor; Donna Florio, Senior Writer; Shirley Harrington, Associate Food Editor

Cover: Triple Chocolate Cake, page 23

contents

W at *Southern Living* are so passionate about chocolate because it goes so well with other Southern favorites like pecans, caramel, bourbon, peanuts, and peanut butter. Serving a chocolate dessert is the ultimate indulgence and highest honor given to guests in some homes. Now you can satisfy all of your chocolate cravings with this mouthwatering collection of over 60 best-of-the-best chocolate recipes. Our chocolate experts at *Southern Living* chose these recipes from the thousands of chocolate recipes we've published over the years.

Of all the favorites that made it into this book, we decided to highlight our top 5 picks. It was tough, but we polled the staff and managed to come up with five contenders to stage a taste test. Scott Jones, Executive Food Editor, hosted 10 chocoholics from across the country in our headquarters building to vote on their

favorites. Scott gave the tasters a bit of the history and details behind each recipe. With plates heaped with scrumptious chocolate desserts, these women had a tough time choosing their favorites, but they obliged.

The top tier below is truly incredible, but we think you'll find all the recipes in the book to be winners.

Top 5 Reasons to Enjoy Chocolate

5. Texas Millionaires, page 108

4. Double Chocolate Cheesecake, page 28

3. Chocolate Cake IV, page 20

2. Chocolate Velvet Cake with Coconut - Pecan Frosting, page 16

1. Chocolate-Bourbon Pecan Pie, page 32

Chocolate Defined

How Chocolate Is Made

Chocolate is grown on cacao trees in the tropics near the equator. The cacao fruit, colorful grooved pods about 12 inches long, grows directly from the trunk and lower branches of the tree. At harvest, the pods are split open and emptied of their pulp and the 24 to 40 navy bean–size seeds. The seeds and pulp are heaped into bins to ferment for three to five days and must be shoveled and turned daily. Without proper fermentation the cocoa beans will not make good chocolate.

Fermented seeds are dried and shipped to chocolate factories where they're cleaned, roasted, and fanned to remove their hulls; next they are broken into pieces called cocoa nibs. Nibs from different varieties and origins are often blended to create chocolates with distinct flavor characteristics, just as grapes are blended in making wine. After blending, the nibs are ground into chocolate liquor, which you know as unsweetened baking chocolate.

How to Handle Chocolate

Storage: Wrap opened chocolate in aluminum foil and then in plastic wrap. Keep it tightly covered in a cool, dry place with low humidity (65° is ideal). In hot weather, you can refrigerate chocolate, but wrap it in foil and seal in a plastic bag so it won't absorb flavors. When bringing refrigerated chocolate to room temperature, leave it wrapped so moisture doesn't condense on it and cause it to seize (stiffen and become lumpy) when melted.

Shelf Life: Chocolate shelf life is determined by the amount of cocoa butter it contains. Unsweetened, semisweet, and bittersweet, if stored properly, will keep for several years. Use milk chocolate within 1 year and white chocolate within 6 months of purchase.

What Is bloom? Chocolate changes color during storage and may take on a gray or grainy appearance called bloom. It happens when chocolate becomes too warm or is exposed to too much moisture.

Melting Chocolate: Chocolate can be melted on the cooktop or in the microwave oven.
• Be sure utensils are dry; even a little water will cause the chocolate to seize or lump.
• On the cooktop, use a heavy pan and low heat.
• To melt in a microwave oven, place 1 cup chocolate pieces or 6 (1-ounce) squares in a microwave-safe measuring cup or bowl. Microwave, uncovered, at MEDIUM (50% power) 2 to 3 minutes or until soft enough to stir until smooth, stirring after 1½ minutes.

Chocolate Choices

shown right, top to bottom
Semisweet chocolate: This real chocolate contains at least 35% chocolate liquor (the liquor qualifying chocolate as real) and 27% cocoa butter. Because it's sold under a variety of names including semisweet, bittersweet, bitter, special dark, dark sweet, and German sweet, buying it can be confusing. In fact, it's possible that a bittersweet chocolate can taste sweeter than a semisweet. Tasting the chocolate is the best way to become familiar with brands of choice.

Dark Chocolate: Also real chocolate as described above, but dark chocolate contains a higher percentage of cocoa butter than semisweet chocolate, 70% or more. Different processing used for dark chocolate also preserves significant amounts of naturally occurring flavonoids that are beneficial to health.

Milk Chocolate: Made of at least 10% chocolate liquor, this real chocolate is recognized by its light color. Its most popular form is the candy bar.

White Chocolate: Contains cocoa butter but is not considered real chocolate because it doesn't contain chocolate liquor. It's extremely sweet and has a buttery mouth feel. Because it's rich in fat, white chocolate is quite perishable, so buy it in small amounts.

Unsweetened: Containing 45% chocolate liquor, the important thing to remember about this real chocolate is that it has no sugar or flavoring added—so don't substitute it for bittersweet or semisweet. This chocolate is used primarily for baking.

Chocolate Morsels: A kitchen staple, morsels can be made from the chocolates mentioned above, and they can also contain added flavors, such as mint, raspberry, or peanut butter. Check labels for specific contents.

Chocolate Flavored Products (not shown): These contain oil rather than cocoa butter and aren't real chocolates. An example is chocolate bark coating.

Chocolate's Good Stuff

1 Calories: A typical dark chocolate bar contains significantly fewer calories and carbs than milk chocolate.

2 Fat: Although it contains saturated fat that's believed to increase LDL, or "bad" cholesterol, new studies reveal that dark chocolate doesn't raise LDL levels. Its high stearic acid content is actually thought to lower serum cholesterol levels.

3 Magnesium: Dark chocolate contains magnesium, known to regulate blood pressure, reducing the risk of heart disease. Magnesium also helps to metabolize the sugar in chocolate—a good double whammy.

4 Antioxidants: Cacao beans (from which chocolate is made) have the highest levels of antioxidants of any known plant source. Antioxidants suppress free radicals, which can damage healthy cells in your body. Dark chocolate has the highest level of cacao solids of any chocolate, making it the best choice of chocolate for your health and fighting disease.

Wine and Chocolate

Pairing wine and chocolate can be the ultimate indulgence. To ensure a flavorful combination, the chocolate should never be sweeter than the wine so that the wine will not taste too sour. Pair lighter, creamier chocolates with light-bodied wines and stronger flavored chocolates with full-bodied wines.

Cabernet Sauvignon: Boasting the classic flavor of dark fruits, this fine red wine is aged in oak barrels for a year or more and then for several more years. With its full-bodied flavor, it pairs nicely with a dark chocolate.

Champagne and Sparkling Wines: With their flavors ranging from dry to sweet and their tasty, oaky aromas, Champagne and sparkling wines both pair well with most types of chocolate. Just remember that all Champagne is sparkling wine, but not all sparkling wine is Champagne. One quality indicator of sparkling wines is the phrase *méthode champenoise*, which means "made in the style of Champagne" on the label.

Chardonnay: Of all the white wine grapes, Chardonnay is perhaps the most popular. Usually dry, Chardonnay has buttery, fruity, vanilla, and toasty flavors. While most white wines are too dry to be served with chocolate, this selection tends to go well with French vanilla chocolate.

Port Wine: Rich, powerful, and oozingly soft, Port is considered the most "masculine" of the famous sweet wines. Deeply berried and chocolaty, Port works best with a dense, creamy chocolate such as a luscious chocolate cheesecake.

Shiraz: Known as Australia's leading red grape variety, Shiraz is also quite popular in America because of its great value and its slightly sweet, full-bodied flavors of black pepper, blackberry, and raspberry. It works well with dark chocolate. It's also typically sought after as an alternative to Cabernet Sauvignon.

Chocolate Fantasies

"Chemically speaking, chocolate really
is the world's perfect food."
—*Michael Levine, nutrition researcher, as quoted in* The Emperors
of Chocolate: Inside the Secret World of Hershey and Mars

Double-Nut Drenched Chocolate Cake

¾ cup butter, softened
2 cups firmly packed light brown sugar
2 large eggs
¾ cup water
¼ cup white vinegar
2 cups all-purpose flour
1 tsp. baking soda

¼ tsp. salt
1 cup finely chopped hazelnuts, toasted
1 Tbsp. vanilla extract
¼ cup unsweetened cocoa
½ cup hazelnut liqueur
Chocolate Topping
Garnish: hazelnuts

1. Grease 3 (8-inch) round cake pans; line bottoms with wax paper. Grease and flour wax paper and sides of pans; set aside.

2. Beat butter at medium speed with an electric mixer until creamy; gradually add brown sugar, beating well. Add eggs, 1 at a time, beating until blended after each addition.

3. Combine water and vinegar. Combine flour, baking soda, and salt; add to butter mixture alternately with water mixture, beginning and ending with flour mixture. Beat at low speed until blended after each addition. Stir in chopped hazelnuts and vanilla. Pour one-third of batter into each of 2 prepared pans. Fold cocoa into remaining batter; pour chocolate batter into third pan.

4. Bake at 350° for 19 to 21 minutes or until a wooden pick inserted in center comes out clean. Cool in pans on wire racks 10 minutes; remove from pans. Peel off wax paper immediately after inverting. Cool completely on wire racks.

5. Brush liqueur over cake layers. Place 1 white cake layer, top side down, on a serving plate; spread one-third of Chocolate Topping over top (do not frost sides). Top with chocolate cake layer; spread one-third Chocolate Topping over chocolate layer (do not frost sides). Top with remaining white cake layer and remaining Chocolate Topping (do not frost sides). Garnish, if desired. Allow cake to set several hours before slicing.

Chocolate Topping

MAKES 5 CUPS

6 (4-oz.) sweet chocolate baking bars, chopped (we tested with Baker's German sweet chocolate)

2 cups butter
1½ cups chopped pecans
2 tsp. vanilla extract

1. Melt chocolate and butter in a heavy saucepan over medium-low heat; cool 10 minutes. Stir in pecans and vanilla; cool until spreading consistency, stirring occasionally (about 45 minutes).

Chocolate Decadence

This heavenly, almost flourless cake was divine enough to make creator chef John Wagner, formerly of Flamingo Cafe in Destin, Florida, famous. Each slice floats in a pool of raspberry sauce and is topped with whipped cream.

2 (8-oz.) packages semisweet chocolate baking squares
⅔ cup butter
5 large eggs

2 Tbsp. sugar
2 Tbsp. all-purpose flour
Raspberry Sauce
Garnishes: whipped cream, fresh raspberries

1. Line bottom of a 9-inch springform pan with parchment paper; set pan aside.

2. Cook chocolate and butter in a heavy saucepan over medium-low heat until melted, stirring occasionally. Beat eggs at medium speed with an electric mixer until blended; gradually add chocolate mixture, beating 10 minutes. Fold in sugar and flour. Pour into prepared pan.

3. Bake at 400° for 15 minutes. (Cake will not be set in center.) Cool 30 minutes. Cover loosely, and chill 8 hours. Spoon about 2½ Tbsp. Raspberry Sauce on each dessert plate; place wedge of chocolate dessert on sauce. Garnish, if desired.

Raspberry Sauce

MAKES 1¾ CUPS

2 cups fresh raspberries
2 cups water
¼ cup sugar

2 Tbsp. cornstarch
2 Tbsp. water

1. Combine raspberries, 2 cups water, and ¼ cup sugar in a large saucepan; bring to a boil. Reduce heat, and simmer, uncovered, 30 minutes. Press raspberry mixture through a wire-mesh strainer, using the back of a spoon to squeeze out juice. Discard pulp and seeds. Return raspberry mixture to saucepan; set aside.

2. Combine cornstarch and 2 Tbsp. water in a small bowl, stirring until smooth; stir into raspberry mixture. Cook over medium heat, stirring constantly, until mixture comes to a boil. Cook 1 more minute, stirring constantly. Remove mixture from heat; cool completely.

Perfect Chocolate Cake

1 cup unsweetened cocoa	2 tsp. baking soda
2 cups boiling water	½ tsp. baking powder
1 cup butter, softened	½ tsp. salt
2½ cups sugar	1½ tsp. vanilla extract
4 large eggs	Whipped Cream Filling
2¾ cups all-purpose flour	Perfect Chocolate Frosting

1. Grease 3 (9-inch) round cake pans; line bottoms with wax paper. Grease and flour wax paper and sides of pans; set aside. Stir together cocoa and 2 cups boiling water until smooth; set aside. Beat butter at medium speed with an electric mixer 2 minutes or until creamy. Gradually add sugar, beating 5 to 7 minutes. Add eggs, 1 at a time, beating just until yellow disappears.

2. Combine flour and next 3 ingredients in a medium bowl; add to butter mixture alternately with cocoa mixture, beginning and ending with flour mixture. Beat at low speed just until blended after each addition. Stir in vanilla. Do not overbeat. Pour batter into prepared pans.

3. Bake at 350° for 22 minutes or until a wooden pick inserted in center comes out clean. Cool in pans on wire racks 10 minutes; remove from pans, and cool completely on wire racks. Spread Whipped Cream Filling between layers; spread Perfect Chocolate Frosting on top and sides of cake. Chill until ready to serve. Store in refrigerator.

Whipped Cream Filling
MAKES ABOUT 2 CUPS

1 cup whipping cream	¼ cup sifted powdered sugar
1 tsp. vanilla extract	

1. Beat cream and vanilla until foamy; gradually add sugar, beating until soft peaks form. Chill.

Perfect Chocolate Frosting
MAKES 2½ CUPS

1 cup semisweet chocolate morsels	¾ cup butter
½ cup half-and-half	2½ cups sifted powdered sugar

1. Combine first 3 ingredients in a medium saucepan; cook over medium heat, stirring until chocolate melts. Remove from heat; whisk in powdered sugar. Place saucepan in a large bowl of ice. Beat at low speed with an electric mixer until frosting holds its shape and loses its gloss. Add a few more drops of half-and-half, if needed, until spreading consistency.

Chocolate Velvet Cake With Coconut-Pecan Frosting

1½ cups semisweet chocolate morsels
½ cup butter, softened
1 (16-oz.) package light brown sugar
3 large eggs
2 cups all-purpose flour
1 tsp. baking soda

½ tsp. salt
1 (8-oz.) container sour cream
1 cup hot water
2 tsp. vanilla extract
Coconut-Pecan Frosting

1. Melt chocolate morsels in a microwave-safe bowl at HIGH 1½ minutes or until melted, stirring at 30-second intervals. Stir until smooth.

2. Beat butter and sugar at medium speed with an electric mixer, beating about 5 minutes or until well blended. Add eggs, 1 at a time, beating just until blended after each addition. Add melted chocolate, beating just until blended.

3. Sift together flour, soda, and salt. Gradually add to chocolate mixture alternately with sour cream, beginning and ending with flour mixture. Beat at low speed just until blended after each addition. Gradually add 1 cup hot water in a slow, steady stream, beating at low speed just until blended. Stir in vanilla.

4. Spoon batter evenly into 3 greased and floured 9-inch round cake pans. Bake at 350° for 25 to 30 minutes or until a wooden pick inserted in center comes out clean. Cool in pans on wire racks 10 minutes. Remove from pans, and let cool completely on wire racks.

5. Spread Coconut-Pecan Frosting between layers and on top and sides of cake.

Coconut-Pecan Frosting

MAKES ABOUT 5 CUPS

1 (12-oz.) can evaporated milk
1½ cups sugar
¾ cup butter or margarine
6 egg yolks

1½ tsp. vanilla extract
2 cups chopped pecans, toasted
1½ cups sweetened flaked coconut

1. Stir together first 4 ingredients in a heavy 3-quart saucepan over medium heat; bring to a boil, and cook, stirring constantly, 12 minutes. Remove from heat; add vanilla, pecans, and coconut, and stir until frosting is cool and spreading consistency.

X-treme Chocolate Double Nut Caramel Ladyfinger Torte

One bite of this confection and your every chocolate dream will be answered. Cream cheese, melted chocolate morsels, and whipped cream team up to make an incredibly smooth filling.

1½ cups semisweet chocolate morsels
2 (3-oz.) packages ladyfingers
1 (13-oz.) jar hazelnut spread (we tested with Nutella)
20 caramels
2⅓ cups whipping cream, divided

1½ cups chopped pecans
⅓ cup powdered sugar
1 (8-oz.) package cream cheese, softened
2 Tbsp. crème de cacao
3 (1-oz.) semisweet chocolate baking squares
2 Tbsp. powdered sugar

1. Microwave chocolate morsels in a microwave-safe bowl at HIGH 1½ minutes or until melted, stirring at 30-second intervals; cool 5 minutes, and set aside.

2. Split ladyfingers, and stand halves around edge of a 9-inch springform pan, placing rounded sides against pan; line bottom of pan with remaining halves. (Reserve remaining ladyfingers for other uses.) Spread hazelnut spread over ladyfingers on bottom of pan.

3. Cook caramels and ⅓ cup whipping cream in a medium saucepan over low heat, stirring constantly, just until melted. Stir in pecans until coated; spoon caramel mixture evenly over hazelnut spread.

4. Beat ⅓ cup powdered sugar and cream cheese in a medium bowl at medium speed with an electric mixer until fluffy. Add crème de cacao, and beat until blended. Beat in melted chocolate morsels until blended.

5. Beat remaining 2 cups whipping cream in a medium bowl at medium speed with an electric mixer until stiff; fold into cream cheese mixture, and spoon evenly over caramel layer in pan.

6. Shave chocolate baking squares with a vegetable peeler evenly on top. Sprinkle evenly with 2 Tbsp. powdered sugar. Chill torte at least 1 hour before serving. Store in refrigerator.

MAKES 12 TO 14 SERVINGS

Chocolate Cake IV

This cake, so named for the four types of chocolate used, will surely go down as one of the best cakes you've ever tried.

Vegetable shortening
½ (4-oz.) semisweet chocolate baking bar, chopped
½ (4-oz.) bittersweet chocolate baking bar, chopped
½ cup butter, softened
2 cups firmly packed light brown sugar
3 large eggs
2 tsp. vanilla extract

2¼ cups cake flour
2 tsp. baking soda
½ tsp. salt
¼ tsp. ground cinnamon
½ cup buttermilk
1 cup boiling water
Coffee Liqueur Ganache Icing
Mocha-Chocolate Cream Filling
Garnish: chocolate curls

1. Coat 3 (8-inch) round cake pans with cooking spray. Line bottoms of pans with wax paper; grease wax paper with shortening, and set aside.

2. Melt chocolate in a small saucepan over low heat, stirring until smooth; set aside.

3. Beat butter at medium speed with an electric mixer until creamy. Gradually add sugar, beating until light and fluffy. Add eggs, 1 at a time, beating just until yellow disappears after each addition. Stir in melted chocolate and vanilla.

4. Sift together flour and next 3 ingredients; add to butter mixture alternately with buttermilk, beating at low speed just until blended, beginning and ending with flour mixture. Stir in boiling water. Pour batter evenly into prepared pans.

5. Bake at 350° for 28 to 30 minutes or until a wooden pick inserted in center comes out clean. Cool in pans on wire racks 10 minutes; remove from pans, and cool completely on wire racks.

6. Place 1 cake layer on a serving plate; spread top with ¼ cup Coffee Liqueur Ganache Icing. Spread half of Mocha-Chocolate Cream Filling evenly over ganache on cake layer. Top with second cake layer; spread top with ¼ cup Coffee Liqueur Ganache Icing and remaining Mocha-Chocolate Cream Filling. Top with remaining cake layer. Spread remaining Coffee Liqueur Ganache Icing on top and sides of cake. Garnish, if desired.

Coffee Liqueur Ganache Icing

MAKES 2 CUPS

3 (4-oz.) bittersweet chocolate baking
    bars, finely chopped
1¼ cups whipping cream

1 Tbsp. butter
2 Tbsp. coffee liqueur

1. Place chocolate in a bowl.

2. Heat cream in a small saucepan over medium heat just until cream begins to boil. Pour over chocolate in bowl, stirring until smooth. Stir in butter and liqueur. Let stand 45 minutes or until spreading consistency.

Mocha-Chocolate Cream Filling

MAKES 1½ CUPS

5 Tbsp. all-purpose flour
2 Tbsp. unsweetened cocoa
2 Tbsp. instant coffee granules
1 cup half-and-half

1 cup butter, softened
1 cup powdered sugar
1 tsp. vanilla extract

1. Whisk together first 4 ingredients in a small saucepan. Cook over medium heat, whisking constantly, 5 minutes or until thickened. Spoon mixture into a small bowl; cover surface of mixture with plastic wrap, pressing wrap onto surface, and let stand 30 minutes or until cool.

2. Beat butter and sugar at medium speed with an electric mixer until light and fluffy. Gradually add cooled cocoa mixture, 1 Tbsp. at a time, beating until blended after each addition. Add vanilla, beating until mixture is consistency of whipped cream.

Ganache is a mixture of chocolate and whipping cream that's heated, cooled to lukewarm, and then poured over a cake like a glaze. Here, it's made slightly thicker so it will spread like a frosting.

shown on page 112

Fudgy Pistachio Bundt Cake

Sour cream and cocoa flavor this moist cake. It has a tender crumb, a thick chocolate glaze, and a sprinkling of pistachios.

1 cup unsweetened cocoa
1 Tbsp. instant coffee granules
1½ cups boiling water
1½ cups butter or margarine, softened
2¼ cups granulated sugar
¾ cup firmly packed brown sugar
5 large eggs
1 (8-oz.) container sour cream
1½ tsp. vanilla extract

2½ cups all-purpose flour
¾ tsp. baking soda
¼ tsp. salt
1 (12-oz.) package semisweet chocolate morsels, divided
¼ cup butter or margarine
3 Tbsp. heavy whipping cream
½ cup chopped pistachio nuts, toasted

1. Combine cocoa, coffee, and boiling water in a bowl, stirring until smooth. Let cool.

2. Beat 1½ cups butter at medium speed with an electric mixer about 2 minutes or until creamy. Gradually add sugars, beating 5 to 7 minutes. Add eggs, 1 at a time, beating just until yellow disappears.

3. Add sour cream and vanilla to cooled cocoa mixture. Combine flour, baking soda, and salt; add to butter mixture alternately with cocoa mixture, beginning and ending with flour mixture. Stir in 1 cup chocolate morsels. Pour batter into a heavily greased and floured 10- x 3½-inch (12-cup) Bundt pan. (Pan will be very full.)

4. Bake at 350° for 1 hour and 5 minutes or until a long wooden pick inserted in center comes out clean. Cool in pan on a wire rack 15 minutes; remove from pan, and cool on wire rack.

5. Meanwhile, combine remaining 1 cup morsels and ¼ cup butter in a small saucepan; cook over low heat until melted. Remove from heat; stir in whipping cream. Let stand 45 minutes.

6. Place cooled cake on rack over wax paper. Pour chocolate glaze over cake; spoon any excess glaze on wax paper over cake. Sprinkle with pistachios.

shown on cover

Triple Chocolate Cake

9 (1-oz.) semisweet chocolate squares
½ cup butter, softened
2 cups granulated sugar
3 large eggs
2 cups all-purpose flour
1 tsp. baking soda
½ tsp. salt

1 (8-oz.) container sour cream
1 cup hot water
2 tsp. vanilla extract
Chocolate Ganache
Chocolate wafer candies (we tested
    wtih Neco)

1. Melt chocolate squares in a microwave-safe bowl at HIGH for 30-second intervals until melted (about 2 minutes total time). Stir until smooth.

2. Beat butter and sugar at medium speed with an electric mixer 5 minutes or until well blended. Add eggs, 1 at a time, beating just until blended after each addition. Add melted chocolate, beating just until blended.

3. Sift together flour, baking soda, and salt. Gradually add flour mixture to chocolate mixture alternately with sour cream, beginning and ending with flour mixture. Beat at low speed just until blended after each addition. Gradually add 1 cup hot water in a slow, steady stream, beating at low speed just until blended. Stir in vanilla.

4. Spoon batter evenly into 3 greased and floured 8-inch round cakepans. Bake at 350° for 25 to 30 minutes or until a wooded pick inserted in center comes out clean. Cool in pans on a wire rack 10 minutes; remove from pans, and let cool completely on wire rack.

5. Spread about ¾ cup Chocolate Ganache between each layer; spread remaining ganache on top and sides of cake. Garnish top and sides of cake with chocolate wafers, if desired.

Chocolate Ganache
MAKES 5½ CUPS

5 cups semisweet chocolate
    morsels

1½ cups heavy whipping cream

1. Microwave chocolate morsels and whipping cream in a microwave-safe bowl at HIGH 1 minute or until chocolate starts to melt; stir until melted and smooth, microwaving again for 30-second intervals, if needed. Let stand 35 minutes or until mixture reaches spreadable consistency, stirring occasionally.

Double Chocolate Bombe

This decadent dome cake boasts both white and dark chocolate mousse fillings sandwiched between thin layers of pecan cake. A rich Chocolate Ganache and sprinkles of chocolate crown it like royalty.

½ cup pecan pieces, toasted
¼ cup butter, softened
¼ cup shortening
1 cup sugar
1½ tsp. vanilla extract
3 large eggs, separated
1 cup all-purpose flour

½ tsp. baking soda
½ cup buttermilk
Chocolate Mousse
White Chocolate Mousse
Chocolate Ganache
Garnish: chocolate curls

1. Process pecans in a food processor until ground; set aside.

2. Beat butter and shortening at medium speed with an electric mixer until creamy; gradually add sugar, beating well. Add vanilla, beating until blended. Add egg yolks, 1 at a time, beating until blended after each addition.

3. Combine flour, soda, and ground pecans; add to sugar mixture alternately with buttermilk, beginning and ending with flour mixture. Beat at low speed until blended after each addition.

4. Beat egg whites until stiff peaks form; fold into batter. Pour into a well-greased and floured 15- x 10-inch jelly-roll pan.

5. Bake at 350° for 20 minutes or until a wooden pick inserted in center comes out clean. Cool in pan on a wire rack 10 minutes; remove from pan, and cool on wire rack.

6. Line a 3-quart mixing bowl (8½ inches across) with plastic wrap. Cut cake lengthwise into 2-inch strips; line prepared bowl with cake strips, reserving remainder. Spread Chocolate Mousse over cake in bowl; cover and chill 1 hour.

7. Pour White Chocolate Mousse into bowl over chocolate layer; cover and chill 1 hour. Cover with remaining strips. Cover and chill at least 8 hours. Invert bombe onto a cake plate, and spread with Chocolate Ganache. Garnish, if desired. Store in refrigerator.

Chocolate Mousse

1 cup whipping cream, divided
1 (8-oz.) package semisweet chocolate baking squares
¼ cup light corn syrup
¼ cup butter
2 Tbsp. powdered sugar
½ tsp. vanilla extract

1. Cook ¼ cup whipping cream and next 3 ingredients in a heavy saucepan over low heat, stirring constantly, until chocolate melts. Cool.

2. Beat remaining ¾ cup whipping cream, powdered sugar, and vanilla at high speed with an electric mixer until stiff peaks form; fold into chocolate mixture. Cover and chill at least 30 minutes.

White Chocolate Mousse

½ cup whipping cream, divided
3 (1-oz.) white chocolate baking squares
2 Tbsp. light corn syrup
2 Tbsp. butter
1 Tbsp. powdered sugar
¼ tsp. vanilla extract

1. Heat 2 Tbsp. whipping cream and next 3 ingredients in a heavy saucepan over low heat, stirring constantly, until smooth. Cool.

2. Beat remaining whipping cream, powdered sugar, and vanilla at high speed with an electric mixer until stiff peaks form; fold into white chocolate mixture.

Chocolate Ganache

1 (8-oz.) package semisweet chocolate baking squares
¼ cup whipping cream

1. Heat chocolate and whipping cream in a heavy saucepan over low heat, stirring constantly, until chocolate melts.

Chocolate Fudge Cheesecake

2 (1-oz.) unsweetened chocolate baking
squares
½ cup butter, softened
1 cup sugar
2 large eggs
½ cup all-purpose flour
½ tsp. vanilla extract
½ cup semisweet chocolate morsels

½ cup chopped pecans, toasted
2 (8-oz.) packages cream cheese, softened
¾ cup sugar
4 large eggs
1 tsp. vanilla extract
Chocolate Glaze
Garnishes: fresh mint sprigs, sliced
strawberries

1. Microwave chocolate squares in a microwave-safe bowl at HIGH 1 minute and 15 seconds, stirring once, or until melted. Stir until smooth.

2. Beat butter and 1 cup sugar at medium speed with an electric mixer until light and fluffy. Add 2 eggs, 1 at a time, beating just until blended after each addition. Add melted chocolate, beating just until blended.

3. Add flour, beating at low speed just until blended. Stir in ½ tsp. vanilla and chocolate morsels.

4. Sprinkle toasted pecans evenly over bottom of a greased and floured 9-inch springform pan. Spoon batter over pecans.

5. Beat cream cheese at medium speed with an electric mixer until smooth; add ¾ cup sugar, beating until blended. Add 4 eggs, 1 at a time, beating just until blended after each addition. Stir in 1 tsp. vanilla. Pour cream cheese mixture over brownie batter.

6. Bake at 325° for 1 hour or until set. Remove from oven, immediately running a knife around edge of pan, releasing sides. Let cool on wire rack. Spread warm Chocolate Glaze over top of cooled cheesecake; cover and chill 8 hours. Remove sides of pan before serving. Garnish, if desired, with fresh mint sprigs and sliced strawberries.

Chocolate Glaze

MAKES ABOUT 1²/₃ CUPS

1 (12-oz.) package semisweet chocolate
morsels

½ cup whipping cream

1. Melt chocolate morsels and whipping cream in a 2-qt. microwave-safe bowl at HIGH 1 minute or until chocolate begins to melt. Whisk until chocolate melts and mixture is smooth.

Double Chocolate Cheesecake

The sweetness of this cheesecake checks in at just the right level to let the chocolate explosion stand out.

1½ cups cream-filled chocolate sandwich cookie crumbs (about 18 cookies)
1 (12-oz.) package semisweet chocolate morsels
3 (8-oz.) packages cream cheese, softened
1 (14-oz.) can sweetened condensed milk
2 tsp. vanilla extract
4 large eggs
Ganache Topping

1. Press cookie crumbs in bottom and halfway up sides of a 9-inch springform pan; set aside.

2. Microwave chocolate morsels in a microwave-safe bowl at HIGH 1½ minutes or until melted, stirring at 30-second intervals.

3. Beat cream cheese at medium speed with an electric mixer 2 minutes or until smooth. Add sweetened condensed milk and vanilla, beating at low speed just until combined. Add eggs, 1 at a time, beating at low speed just until blended after each addition. Add melted chocolate, beating just until combined. Pour cheesecake batter into prepared crust.

4. Bake at 300° for 1 hour and 5 minutes or just until center is set. Turn off oven. Let cheesecake stand in oven 30 minutes with oven door closed. Remove cheesecake from oven; run a knife along outer edge of cheesecake to loosen, and cool in pan on a wire rack until room temperature. Cover and chill 8 hours.

5. Remove sides of springform pan, and place cake on a serving plate. Slowly pour and spread warm Ganache Topping over cheesecake, letting it run down sides of cheesecake. Chill 1 hour before serving. Store in refrigerator.

Ganache Topping

MAKES 1½ CUPS

¾ cup whipping cream
1 cup semisweet chocolate morsels
1 cup milk chocolate morsels

1. Bring cream to a boil in a saucepan over medium heat; quickly remove from heat, and stir in semisweet and milk chocolate morsels until melted and smooth. Let mixture cool until slightly warm (about 30 minutes) before pouring and spreading over cheesecake.

Molten Chocolate Cakes

These yummy little cakes ooze soft chocolate from their centers when you spoon into them.

2 Tbsp. butter, melted
2 Tbsp. unsweetened cocoa
¾ cup butter, cut into pieces
3 (4-oz.) bars premium semisweet chocolate, broken into chunks (we tested with Ghirardelli)

½ cup whipping cream
1¼ cups egg substitute (see Note)
¾ cup granulated sugar
⅔ cup all-purpose flour
Powdered sugar

1. Brush 16 muffin cups with 2 Tbsp. melted butter. Sprinkle evenly with cocoa, shaking out excess. Place in refrigerator to firm butter.

2. Place ¾ cup butter and chocolate in a large heavy saucepan. Cook over low heat, stirring often, until butter and chocolate melt. Slowly whisk in cream; set aside.

3. Combine egg substitute and sugar in a large mixing bowl. Beat at medium speed with an electric mixer 5 to 7 minutes or until slightly thickened; add chocolate cream and flour, beating until blended. Pour batter into muffin cups, filling to within ¼ inch from tops. Cover and chill at least 1 hour or up to 24 hours.

4. Bake at 450° for 10 to 11 minutes or just until edges of cakes spring back when lightly touched but centers are still soft. Let stand 3 minutes before loosening edges with a knife. Quickly invert cakes onto a baking sheet. Transfer to dessert plates using a spatula. Sprinkle with powdered sugar. Serve warm.

Note: The recipe uses egg substitute instead of real eggs because the cakes aren't in the oven long enough for eggs to cook thoroughly.

Mocha-Pecan Mud Pie

This dessert is so rich your guests will never know it uses
several light products.

½ cup chopped pecans
1 tsp. sugar
1 pt. light coffee ice cream, softened
(we tested with Häagen-Dazs Light
Coffee Ice Cream)
1 pt. light chocolate ice cream, softened
(we tested with Häagen-Dazs Light
Dutch Chocolate Ice Cream)

1 cup coarsely chopped reduced-fat
cream-filled chocolate sandwich
cookies, divided (about 10 cookies)
1 (6-oz.) ready-made chocolate crumb
piecrust (we tested with Keebler
Chocolate Ready Crust)
2 Tbsp. light chocolate syrup

1. Place pecans in a single layer on a baking sheet coated with cooking spray; sprinkle evenly
with sugar. Bake at 350° for 8 to 10 minutes or until lightly toasted. Cool.

2. Stir together ice cream, ¾ cup cookie chunks, and ⅓ cup pecans; spoon into piecrust.
Freeze 10 minutes.

3. Press remaining cookie chunks and pecans evenly on top. Cover with plastic wrap, and
freeze 8 hours. Drizzle individual slices with chocolate syrup.

"Make a list of important things to
do today, and put 'eat chocolate' on it. Now,
you'll get at least one thing done today."
—Gina Hays

Chocolate-Bourbon Pecan Pie

Serve a decadent wedge of perfection warm or chilled with a dollop of whipped cream or ice cream.

½ (15-oz.) package refrigerated piecrusts
1½ cups chopped pecans
1 cup semisweet chocolate morsels
1 cup dark corn syrup
½ cup granulated sugar
½ cup firmly packed brown sugar

¼ cup bourbon or water
4 large eggs
¼ cup butter or margarine, melted
2 tsp. cornmeal
2 tsp. vanilla extract
½ tsp. salt

1. Fit piecrust into a 9-inch deep-dish pieplate according to package directions; fold edges under, and crimp.

2. Sprinkle pecans and chocolate evenly into piecrust; set aside.

3. Combine corn syrup and next 3 ingredients in a large saucepan, and bring to a boil over medium heat. Cook, stirring constantly, 3 minutes. Remove from heat.

4. Whisk together eggs and next 4 ingredients. Gradually whisk about one-fourth of hot mixture into egg mixture; add to remaining hot mixture, whisking constantly. Pour filling into prepared piecrust.

5. Bake at 325° for 55 minutes or until set; cool on a wire rack.

Sweetheart Fudge Pie

This incredible pie is so rich and fudgy it easily serves eight chocoholics.

½ cup butter or margarine, softened
¾ cup firmly packed brown sugar
3 large eggs
1 (12-oz.) package semisweet chocolate morsels, melted
2 tsp. instant coffee granules

1 tsp. rum extract
½ cup all-purpose flour
1 cup coarsely chopped walnuts
1 unbaked 9-inch pastry shell
Garnishes: whipped cream, chopped walnuts

1. Beat butter at medium speed with an electric mixer until creamy; gradually add brown sugar, beating well. Add eggs, 1 at a time, beating until blended after each addition. Add melted chocolate, coffee granules, and rum extract; mix well. Stir in flour and 1 cup chopped walnuts. Pour into shell.

2. Bake at 375° for 25 minutes; cool completely. Cover and chill 8 hours. Garnish, if desired.

"I have a theory that chocolate slows the aging process.... It may not be true, but do I dare take the chance?"—*Unknown*

Chocolate Chunk Bread Pudding With White Chocolate Brandy Sauce

Chunks of half-melted chocolate appear in every bite of this sinfully good bread pudding. And it gets even better—you serve it in a pool of brandy sauce.

1 (1-lb.) loaf day-old French bread
3½ cups milk
1 cup half-and-half
4 large eggs, lightly beaten
1 cup sugar
2 Tbsp. butter or margarine, melted
1 Tbsp. vanilla extract
⅛ tsp. salt
2 (4-oz.) bittersweet chocolate baking bars, chopped (we tested with Ghirardelli)
White Chocolate Brandy Sauce

1. Tear bread into small pieces; place in a large bowl. Add milk and half-and-half; let mixture stand 10 minutes.

2. Combine eggs, sugar, butter, vanilla, and salt; add to bread, stirring well. Stir in chopped chocolate. Spoon mixture into a lightly greased 13- x 9-inch pan. Bake, uncovered, at 325° for 55 minutes or until firm and lightly browned. Serve warm with warm White Chocolate Brandy Sauce.

White Chocolate Brandy Sauce

MAKES 1¾ CUPS

½ cup sugar
½ cup butter or margarine
½ cup half-and-half
1 (4-oz.) white chocolate baking bar (we tested with Ghirardelli)
3 Tbsp. brandy

1. Combine first 3 ingredients in a saucepan; bring to a boil over medium heat, stirring until sugar dissolves. Reduce heat, and simmer 5 minutes. Remove from heat; add white chocolate, stirring until chocolate melts. Stir in brandy. Serve warm.

Everyday Indulgences

"All I really need is love, but a little chocolate now and then doesn't hurt!"

—*Lucy Van Pelt*, Charles M. Schulz's *Peanuts*

Chocolate Candy Cupcakes

1 cup unsalted butter, softened
1 ¼ cups granulated sugar
¾ cup packed light brown sugar
4 large eggs
1 cup semisweet chocolate morsels, melted
1 cup buttermilk
1 teaspoon vanilla extract
½ teaspoon chocolate extract

2 cups all-purpose flour
1 teaspoon baking soda
¼ teaspoon salt
Chocolate Ganache
Garnishes: Snow Caps, chocolate covered espresso beans, and white chocolate chips

1. Beat butter and sugars at medium speed with an electric mixer 3 minutes or until creamy. Add eggs, 1 at a time, beating just until yellow disappears. Add melted chocolate, beating until blended.

2. Combine buttermilk and extracts in a small bowl. Combine flour, soda, and salt; add to butter mixture alternately with buttermilk mixture, beginning and ending with flour mixture. Beat at low speed until blended after each addition. Spoon batter into paper-lined muffin pans, filling between one-half and two-thirds full.

3. Bake at 350° for 20 minutes or until a wooden pick inserted in center comes out clean. Remove from pans, and cool completely on wire racks. Spread evenly with Chocolate Ganache. Garnish, if desired.

Chocolate Ganache
MAKES 2 ¾ CUPS

2 ½ cups semisweet chocolate morsels
¾ cup heavy whipping cream

1. Microwave chocolate morsels and whipping cream in a microwave-safe bowl at HIGH 1 minute or until chocolate begins to melt; stir until melted and smooth.

2. Let stand 25 minutes or until mixture reaches spreadable consistency, stirring occasionally.

shown on page 36

Mississippi Mud Cake

Everyone loves this sheet cake. It's perfect for casual gatherings because it's quick to make and easy to transport. It's also a dream to devour!

1 cup butter, melted	⅛ tsp. salt
2 cups sugar	1½ cups all-purpose flour
½ cup unsweetened cocoa	1½ cups coarsely chopped pecans, toasted
4 large eggs, lightly beaten	1 (10.5-oz.) bag miniature marshmallows
1 tsp. vanilla extract	Chocolate Frosting

1. Whisk together first 6 ingredients in a large bowl. Stir in flour and chopped pecans. Pour batter into a greased and floured 15- x 10-inch jelly-roll pan.

2. Bake at 350° for 20 to 25 minutes or until a wooden pick inserted in center comes out clean. Remove from oven; top warm cake evenly with marshmallows. Return to oven, and bake 5 minutes. Drizzle Chocolate Frosting over warm cake. Cool completely.

Note: Substitute 2 (19.5-oz.) packages brownie mix, prepared according to package directions, for first 7 ingredients, if desired. Stir in chopped pecans. Bake at 350° for 30 minutes. Proceed with marshmallows and frosting as directed.

Chocolate Frosting

MAKES 2 CUPS

1 (16-oz.) package powdered sugar, sifted	¼ cup butter, softened
½ cup milk	⅓ cup unsweetened cocoa

1. Beat all ingredients at medium speed with an electric mixer until smooth.

Texas Sheet Cake

Our staff couldn't get enough of this cake we adapted from *The Texas Holiday Cookbook* (Gulf Publishing, 1997) and *The Contemporary Cowboy Cookbook: Recipes From the Wild West to Wall Street* (Taylor Trade Publishing, 2004), by Dotty Griffith of Dallas, Texas. Make the icing 5 minutes before taking the cake out of the oven, and spread it on the hot cake.

2 cups sugar
2 cups all-purpose flour
½ cup butter
½ cup shortening
¼ cup unsweetened cocoa
1 cup water

½ cup buttermilk
2 large eggs, lightly beaten
1 tsp. baking soda
1 tsp. vanilla extract
Chocolate Icing

1. Sift together sugar and flour in a large bowl; set aside. Stir together butter and next 3 ingredients in a medium saucepan over medium heat, stirring constantly, 5 minutes or just until butter and shortening melt. Remove from heat, and pour over sugar mixture, stirring until dissolved. Cool slightly.

2. Stir in buttermilk and next 3 ingredients. Pour into a greased and lightly floured 15- x 10-inch jelly-roll pan. Bake at 400° for 20 minutes. (Cake will have a fudgelike texture.) Spread hot cake with Chocolate Icing.

Chocolate Icing

MAKES ABOUT 4 CUPS

½ cup butter
¼ cup unsweetened cocoa
⅓ cup milk

1 (16-oz.) package powdered sugar
1 tsp. vanilla extract
1 cup chopped pecans

1. Combine butter, cocoa, and milk in a medium saucepan. Cook over low heat 5 minutes or until butter melts. Bring to a boil over medium heat. Remove from heat; stir in sugar, vanilla, and pecans. Beat at medium speed with an electric mixer until mixture is smooth and sugar dissolves.

Chocolate-Praline Pecan Cake

Make sure your 9-inch square pans are at least 2 inches deep.
If your pans are on the shallow side, all the batter won't fit.

1½ cups semisweet chocolate morsels	1 cup hot water
½ cup butter, softened	4 tsp. vanilla extract, divided
1 (16-oz.) package light brown sugar	2 cups firmly packed brown sugar
3 large eggs	⅔ cup whipping cream
2 cups all-purpose flour	½ cup butter
1 tsp. baking soda	2 cups powdered sugar, sifted
½ tsp. salt	2 cups chopped pecans, toasted
1 (8-oz.) container sour cream	

1. Melt chocolate morsels in a microwave-safe bowl at HIGH for 30-second intervals until melted (about 1½ minutes total time). Stir until smooth.

2. Beat ½ cup softened butter and 16 oz. brown sugar at medium speed with an electric mixer about 5 minutes or until well blended. Add eggs, 1 at a time, just until blended after each addition. Add melted chocolate, beating just until blended.

3. Sift together flour, soda, and salt. Gradually add to chocolate mixture alternately with sour cream, beginning and ending with flour mixture. Beat at low speed just until blended after each addition. Gradually add 1 cup hot water in a slow, steady stream, beating at low speed just until blended. Stir in 2 tsp. vanilla.

4. Spoon batter evenly into 2 greased and floured aluminum foil-lined 9- x 9- inch square pans. Bake at 350° for 40 minutes or until a wooden pick inserted in center comes out clean. Cool in pans on wire racks.

5. Bring 2 cups brown sugar, whipping cream, and ½ cup butter to a boil in a 3-quart saucepan over medium heat, stirring often; boil 1 minute. Remove from heat; whisk in powdered sugar and remaining 2 tsp. vanilla. Add pecans, stirring gently 3 to 5 minutes or until mixture begins to cool and thicken slightly. Pour immediately over cakes in pans. Cool completely. Cut into squares.

Chocolate Velvet "Pound" Cake

Ice cream and warm Chocolate Ganache (recipe on page 47) go perfectly with this moist and tender cake.

1½ cups semisweet chocolate morsels
½ cup butter, softened
1 (16-oz.) package light brown sugar
3 large eggs
2 cups all-purpose flour
1 tsp. baking soda

½ tsp. salt
1 (8-oz.) container sour cream
1 cup hot water
2 tsp. vanilla extract
¼ cup powdered sugar

1. Melt chocolate morsels in a microwave-safe bowl at HIGH for 30-second intervals until melted (about 1½ minutes total time). Stir until smooth.

2. Beat butter and brown sugar at medium speed with an electric mixer about 5 minutes or until well blended. Add eggs, 1 at a time, beating just until blended after each addition. Add melted chocolate, beating just until blended.

3. Sift together flour, baking soda, and salt. Gradually add to chocolate mixture alternately with sour cream, beginning and ending with flour mixture. Beat at low speed just until blended after each addition. Gradually add 1 cup hot water in a slow steady stream, beating at low speed just until blended. Stir in vanilla.

4. Spoon batter evenly into a greased and floured 10-inch tube pan. Bake at 350° for 55 to 65 minutes or until a wooden pick inserted in center comes out clean. Cool in pan on a wire rack 10 minutes. Remove from pan, and let cool completely on wire rack.

5. Sift powdered sugar over top of cake.

Chocolate Cake With Buttercream Mint Frosting

Don't be tempted to substitute peppermint extract for the peppermint oil used in this frosting recipe. Peppermint oil, available from cake-supply stores, has an intense, highly concentrated flavor like that found in chocolate-covered peppermint patties. It "takes the cake," shall we say?

1½ cups semisweet chocolate morsels
½ cup butter, softened
1 (16-oz.) package light brown sugar
3 large eggs
2 cups all-purpose flour
1 tsp. baking soda
½ tsp. salt
1 (8-oz.) container sour cream
1 cup hot water
2 tsp. vanilla extract
Buttercream Mint Frosting
Chocolate Ganache

1. Melt chocolate morsels in a microwave-safe bowl at HIGH for 30-second intervals until melted (about 1½ minutes total time). Stir until smooth.

2. Beat butter and sugar at medium speed with an electric mixer, about 5 minutes or until well blended. Add eggs, 1 at a time, beating just until blended after each addition. Add melted chocolate, beating just until blended.

3. Sift together flour, soda, and salt. Gradually add to chocolate mixture alternately with sour cream, beginning and ending with flour mixture. Beat at low speed just until blended after each addition. Gradually add 1 cup hot water in a slow, steady stream, beating at low speed just until blended. Stir in vanilla.

4. Spoon batter evenly into 3 well-greased and floured 9-inch round cake pans. Bake at 350° for 28 to 30 minutes or until a wooden pick inserted in center of cake comes out clean. Cool in pans on wire racks 10 minutes; remove from pans, and let cool completely on wire racks.

5. Spread Buttercream Mint Frosting evenly between cake layers. Spread Chocolate Ganache evenly over top and sides of cake.

Buttercream Mint Frosting

½ cup butter, softened
1 (16-oz.) package powdered sugar
⅓ cup milk

1½ tsp. vanilla extract
½ tsp. peppermint oil

1. Beat butter at medium speed with an electric mixer until creamy; gradually add powdered sugar alternately with milk, beating at low speed until blended after each addition. Stir in vanilla and peppermint oil.

Chocolate Ganache

1 (12-oz.) package semisweet chocolate morsels

½ cup whipping cream
3 Tbsp. butter

1. Microwave chocolate morsels and whipping cream in a 2-qt. microwave-safe bowl at MEDIUM (50% power) 2 minutes or until chocolate begins to melt.

2. Whisk until chocolate melts and mixture is smooth. Whisk in butter; let stand 20 minutes. Beat at medium speed with an electric mixer 3 to 4 minutes or until mixture forms soft peaks.

"Strength is the capacity to break a chocolate bar into four pieces with your bare hands and then just eat one of the pieces."

—Judith Viorst

Fudge Spoon Pie

This dessert is too rich and gooey to slice like a pie—spoon it out like a cobbler, and top it with your favorite ice cream.

½ cup butter
1 (1-oz.) square unsweetened chocolate
1 cup sugar
½ cup all-purpose flour

1 tsp. vanilla extract
2 large eggs, lightly beaten
Ice cream

1. Melt butter and chocolate in a saucepan over low heat, stirring often; remove from heat. Stir in sugar and next 3 ingredients.

2. Pour batter into a greased 8-inch square pan. Bake at 325° for 22 minutes. (Do not over-bake.) Serve warm with ice cream.

When melting chocolate, it's best to remove it from heat when it appears about two-thirds melted. Continue stirring until completely melted.

No-Bake Chocolate Chip Cookie Pie

Milk and cookies come together to form this simple pie. Dunk cookies in milk, and layer them in the crust with whipped topping. As the pie chills, the moist layers become a yummy filling.

1 (15- or 18-oz.) package chocolate chip cookies*

1 cup milk

1 (9-oz.) commercial graham cracker crust (extra serving size)

1 (8-oz.) container frozen whipped topping, thawed

1. Dip 8 cookies in milk, and place in a single layer in graham cracker crust. Top with one-third of whipped topping. Dip 8 more cookies in milk; place on top; spread with one-third of whipped topping. Repeat layers with 8 more cookies, milk, and remaining whipped topping. Crumble 2 chocolate chip cookies, and sprinkle over pie. Cover and chill 8 hours before serving.

*For cookies, we used Nabisco Chunky Chips Ahoy. You'll need 26 cookies for this recipe (you may have a few leftover cookies in the package).

"In the cookies of life, friends are the chocolate chips." —*Unknown*

Mildred's Toffee

This classic recipe takes less than 30 minutes and is almost as easy as boiling water. We loved the recipe so much we added a couple of nut variations and a splash of spirits.

1¹⁄₂ cups chopped toasted pecans, divided
  1 cup sugar
  1 cup butter

1 Tbsp. light corn syrup
¹⁄₄ cup water
1 cup semisweet chocolate morsels

1. Spread 1 cup pecans in a 9-inch circle on a lightly greased baking sheet.

2. Bring sugar and next 3 ingredients to a boil in a heavy saucepan over medium heat, stirring constantly. Cook until mixture is golden brown and a candy thermometer registers 290° to 310° (about 15 minutes). Pour sugar mixture over pecans on baking sheet.

3. Sprinkle with morsels; let stand 30 seconds. Spread melted morsels evenly over top; sprinkle with remaining ¹⁄₂ cup chopped pecans. Chill 1 hour. Break into bite-size pieces. Store in an airtight container.

Almond Toffee
Substitute 1 cup chopped toasted slivered almonds for 1 cup chopped pecans to sprinkle on baking sheet. Substitute ¹⁄₂ cup toasted sliced almonds for ¹⁄₂ cup chopped pecans to sprinkle over chocolate. Proceed as directed.

Hawaiian Toffee
Substitute 1 cup chopped toasted macadamia nuts for 1 cup chopped pecans to sprinkle on baking sheet. Substitute ¹⁄₂ cup toasted sweetened flaked coconut for ¹⁄₂ cup chopped pecans to sprinkle over chocolate. Proceed as directed.

Bourbon-Pecan Toffee
Substitute ¹⁄₄ cup bourbon for ¹⁄₄ cup water. Proceed as directed.

Mocha Ice Cream

You'll savor every frosty spoonful of this rich and ultra-creamy ice cream. Make it ahead and freeze it indoors after its turn in the traditional ice-cream freezer, if you'd like.

1 (8-oz.) package semisweet chocolate squares, coarsely chopped	1 cup half-and-half
¼ cup strong brewed coffee	¾ cup sugar, divided
2 cups whipping cream	3 Tbsp. instant coffee granules
	4 egg yolks

1. Microwave chocolate in a 1-quart microwave-safe bowl at HIGH 1½ minutes or until melted, stirring twice; stir in brewed coffee. Set chocolate mixture aside.

2. Bring whipping cream, half-and-half, ½ cup sugar, and coffee granules to a boil in a heavy saucepan over medium-high heat, stirring until sugar and coffee dissolve.

3. Beat yolks and remaining ¼ cup sugar at high speed with an electric mixer until thick and pale. With mixer at low speed, gradually pour hot cream mixture into yolk mixture; return to saucepan.

4. Cook over medium heat, stirring constantly, 6 to 8 minutes or until mixture thickens and coats a spoon. Remove from heat; stir in chocolate mixture. Cover and chill at least 2 hours.

5. Pour chilled mixture into freezer container of a 5-quart hand-turned or electric freezer. Freeze according to manufacturer's instructions.

6. Pack freezer with additional ice and rock salt; let stand 1 hour.

The ice cream will keep up to a month if stored in the freezer in a tightly sealed container.

Chocolate Cookie Ice Cream

Make your own cookies 'n' cream ice cream with these three ingredients, which you probably have on hand.

1 (16-oz.) package cream-filled chocolate sandwich cookies, coarsely crumbled (42 cookies)

½ gal. vanilla ice cream, slightly softened
1 (8-oz.) container frozen whipped topping, thawed

1. Combine crumbled cookies and softened ice cream, stirring just until blended. Fold in whipped topping. Spoon mixture into a 13- x 9-inch pan or other large shallow container. Cover and freeze until firm. Scoop into serving bowls.

To soften ice cream for this recipe, let it stand at room temperature for 20 to 30 minutes.

Chocolate Chubbies

You can't go wrong with this much chocolate and nuts in these candylike cookies. These sensational treats were adapted from Decatur, Alabama, cooking teacher and caterer Betty Sims's book *Southern Scrumptious: How to Cater Your Own Party* (Betty Sims, 1997).

6 (1-oz.) semisweet chocolate squares, chopped
2 (1-oz.) unsweetened chocolate squares, chopped
⅓ cup butter
3 large eggs
1 cup sugar
¼ cup all-purpose flour
½ tsp. baking powder
⅛ tsp. salt
1 (12-oz.) package semisweet chocolate morsels
2 cups coarsely chopped pecans
2 cups coarsely chopped walnuts

1. Combine first 3 ingredients in a heavy saucepan; cook, stirring often, over low heat until chocolate melts. Remove from heat; cool slightly.

2. Beat eggs and sugar at medium speed with an electric mixer until smooth; add chocolate mixture, beating well.

3. Combine flour, baking powder, and salt; add to chocolate mixture, stirring just until dry ingredients are moistened. Fold in chocolate morsels, pecans, and walnuts.

4. Drop batter by tablespoonfuls 2 inches apart onto lightly greased baking sheets.

5. Bake at 325° for 12 to 15 minutes or until done. Cool cookies on baking sheets 1 minute. Remove to wire racks; cool.

Gooey Turtle Bars

No bowls needed! Combine crust ingredients right in the pan; then sprinkle and drizzle toppings. Cleanup is easy with this recipe.

2 cups graham cracker crumbs or vanilla
   wafer crumbs
½ cup butter or margarine, melted
1 (12-oz.) package semisweet chocolate
   morsels

1 cup pecan pieces
1 (12-oz.) jar caramel topping

1. Combine crumbs and butter in an ungreased 13- x 9-inch pan; stir and press firmly in bottom of pan. Sprinkle with chocolate morsels and pecans.

2. Remove lid from caramel topping; microwave at HIGH 1 to 1½ minutes or until hot, stirring after 30 seconds. Drizzle over pecans. Bake at 350° for 15 minutes or until morsels melt; let cool in pan on a wire rack. Chill at least 30 minutes; cut into bars.

"If it ain't chocolate, it ain't breakfast."

—*Unknown*

Double Chocolate Espresso Brownies

Wow everyone with a tower of brownie cutouts. Drizzle with
fudge sauce, and use tongs for serving.

1¼ cups all-purpose flour
¼ tsp. baking soda
⅛ tsp. baking powder
⅛ tsp. salt
14 (1-oz.) semisweet chocolate squares,
   finely chopped
 1 cup sugar
½ cup butter

¼ cup light corn syrup
¼ cup brewed espresso or French roast
   coffee
 3 large eggs
 1 Tbsp. vanilla extract
 1 cup coarsely chopped walnuts
 6 oz. premium Swiss dark chocolate or
   milk chocolate, coarsely chopped

1. Coat a 13- x 9-inch pan with cooking spray. Line pan with aluminum foil, allowing ends
to hang over short sides of pan. Tuck overlapping ends under rim on short sides. Coat foil
with cooking spray; set pan aside.

2. Combine flour and next 3 ingredients in a small bowl. Place chopped semisweet chocolate
in a large bowl; set bowls aside.

3. Combine sugar and next 3 ingredients in a saucepan. Cook over medium heat, stirring
constantly, until sugar and butter melt and mixture comes to a rolling boil. Remove from
heat, and pour over chopped chocolate in bowl; let stand 2 minutes (do not stir).

4. Beat chocolate mixture at low speed with an electric mixer until chocolate melts and mixture is smooth. Add eggs, 1 at a time, beating well after each addition. Add flour mixture;
beat at medium speed until well blended. Stir in vanilla, walnuts, and dark chocolate. Spoon
batter into prepared pan, spreading evenly.

5. Bake at 325° for 38 to 40 minutes. Cool completely in pan on a wire rack. Cover and chill
at least 2 hours.

6. Carefully invert brownies from pan, using overlapping foil as handles; remove foil. Invert
brownies again onto a cutting board; cut into squares or circles. (We used a 2½-inch round
cutter. There'll be some fudgy scraps left for nibbling or topping ice cream.)

Heavenly Chocolate Chunk Cookies

Chocolate chunks give a big chocolate taste to every bite of these deluxe chocolate chip cookies.

2 cups plus 2 Tbsp. all-purpose flour
½ tsp. baking soda
½ tsp. salt
¾ cup butter or margarine
2 Tbsp. instant coffee granules
1 cup firmly packed brown sugar

½ cup granulated sugar
1 large egg
1 egg yolk
1 (11.5-oz.) package semisweet chocolate chunks
1 cup walnut halves, toasted

1. Combine first 3 ingredients; stir well.

2. Combine butter and coffee granules in a small saucepan or skillet. Cook over medium-low heat until butter melts and coffee granules dissolve, stirring occasionally. Remove from heat, and let cool to room temperature. (Don't let butter resolidify.)

3. Combine butter mixture, sugars, egg, and egg yolk in a large bowl. Beat at medium speed with an electric mixer until blended. Gradually add flour mixture, beating at low speed just until blended. Stir in chocolate chunks and walnuts.

4. Drop dough by heaping tablespoonfuls 2 inches apart onto ungreased baking sheets. Bake at 325° for 12 to 14 minutes. Let cool slightly on baking sheets. Remove to wire racks to cool completely.

Toffee Cookie Bites

The saltine crackers in this easy-to-make recipe marry salty with sweet.

24 saltine crackers
 1 cup butter
 1 cup firmly packed light brown sugar
 1 (11.5 or 12-oz.) package milk
    chocolate morsels

½ cup chopped pecans or walnuts,
    toasted

1. Cover bottom of a 13- x 9-inch aluminum foil-lined pan with crackers.

2. Microwave butter and brown sugar in a microwave-safe glass bowl at HIGH 3 to 4 minutes or until sugar dissolves, stirring occasionally. Pour butter mixture over crackers.

3. Bake at 325° for 15 minutes or until bubbly. Remove from oven, and sprinkle with chocolate morsels, spreading as they melt. Sprinkle with pecans.

4. Cover and chill at least 2 hours. Cut toffee into 1-inch squares, or break into pieces, and store in an airtight container in refrigerator.

"Nuts just take up space where the chocolate ought to be."—*Unknown*

Chocolate Cookie Pudding

We loved this pudding so much that we came up with another scrumptious version by making a couple of substitutions.

1 (5.9-oz.) package chocolate instant pudding mix
2 cups milk
1 (3-oz.) package cream cheese, softened
1 (8-oz.) container frozen whipped topping, thawed

16 double-stuffed cream-filled chocolate sandwich cookies, crushed (about 2 cups) (we tested with Oreo Double Stuf)
¾ cup chopped pecans, toasted

1. Whisk together chocolate instant pudding mix and 2 cups milk for 2 minutes. Cover pudding, and chill 5 minutes.

2. Stir together cream cheese and whipped topping, blending well.

3. Place 1 cup crushed cookies in an 8-cup bowl. Spread half of cream cheese mixture over crushed cookies; sprinkle with half of pecans. Spread all of pudding evenly over top; spread remaining cream cheese mixture evenly over pudding. Sprinkle with remaining cookies and pecans. Chill until ready to serve.

Chocolate-Peanut Butter Cookie Pudding

Crush 16 peanut butter cream-filled chocolate sandwich cookies (we tested with Double Delight Oreo Peanut Butter & Chocolate). Substitute ¼ cup creamy peanut butter for cream cheese and 1 cup chopped dry roasted peanuts for pecans. Proceed as directed.

Jump-Start Jewels

"I could give up chocolate,
but I'm not a quitter."

—*Unknown*

shown on page 64

Peanut Butter-Brownie Trifle

Chocolate, peanut butter, and whipping cream—here's perfection in a trifle bowl. Dig deeply to get all the luscious layers when you dish this out.

1 (19-oz.) package fudge brownie mix*
2 cups whipping cream, divided
1 (10-oz.) package peanut butter & milk chocolate morsels
2 tsp. vanilla extract
1½ cups peanut butter candy, chopped (we tested with Nestlé Treasures)

1 (8-oz.) container frozen whipped topping, thawed
1 (10-oz.) package peanut butter & milk chocolate morsels (optional)

1. Prepare and bake brownie mix according to package directions in a 13- x 9-inch pan; cool. Cut into 2-inch squares.

2. Cook ⅔ cup whipping cream and 1 package of morsels in a small saucepan over low heat, stirring constantly until blended; remove from heat, and stir in vanilla. Chill 30 minutes.

3. Beat remaining 1⅓ cups whipping cream at high speed with an electric mixer until soft peaks form. Stir one-third of whipped cream into chocolate mixture. Fold in remaining whipped cream.

4. Layer half of brownies in a 3½-quart trifle dish or bowl; top with half of chocolate mixture, half of chopped peanut butter candy, and half of whipped topping. Repeat procedure with remaining brownies, chocolate mixture, chopped peanut butter candy, and whipped topping.

5. Sprinkle other package of morsels in an even layer on a parchment- or wax paper-lined 13- x 9-inch pan. Bake at 200° for 2 minutes or until morsels are evenly melted. Spread with a spatula to swirl chocolate; chill 1 hour or until firm. Break into pieces. Garnish trifle with peanut butter-chocolate pieces, if desired. Store trifle in refrigerator.

*Substitute 2 (18-oz.) packages refrigerated fudgy brownie bar dough for brownie mix. Prepare and bake according to package directions.

German Chocolate Cake

A homemade frosting jazzes up cake mix for this easy snack cake version of a favorite layer cake. You can substitute light sour cream in this recipe, but don't use nonfat sour cream.

1 (18.25-oz.) package German chocolate cake mix (we tested with Betty Crocker Super Moist German Chocolate Cake Mix)

3 large eggs
1 (8-oz.) container sour cream
1/3 cup vegetable oil
Coconut-Pecan Filling

1. Beat first 4 ingredients at low speed with an electric mixer 30 seconds or just until moistened; beat mixture at medium speed 2 minutes. Pour batter evenly into a greased and floured 13- x 9-inch pan.

2. Bake at 350° for 32 to 35 minutes or until a wooden pick inserted in center comes out clean. Cool cake completely in pan on a wire rack.

3. Spread Coconut-Pecan Filling evenly on top of cake.

Coconut-Pecan Filling

MAKES ABOUT 3 CUPS

1 cup sugar
1 cup whipping cream
3 egg yolks
1/2 cup butter

1 tsp. vanilla extract
1 1/3 cups sweetened flaked coconut
1 cup chopped pecans, toasted

1. Combine first 4 ingredients in a medium saucepan; cook over medium heat, stirring constantly, 8 to 10 minutes or until thickened. Remove from heat, and stir in vanilla. Stir in coconut and pecans, and let cool completely.

Mocha Brownie Cake

We baked brownie mix in two cake pans and then stacked and lavished them with mocha cream frosting. It's a short, brownie-like cake with wonderful texture contrasts. Chilling this dessert gives the coffee-cream filling time to set, and it makes the cake easier to slice and serve.

1 (21-oz.) package chewy fudge brownie mix (we tested with Duncan Hines Brownie Mix)
¼ cup water
½ cup vegetable oil
3 large eggs, lightly beaten

½ cup chopped pecans
1½ cups heavy whipping cream
1 Tbsp. instant coffee granules
¼ cup sifted powdered sugar
Garnish: chocolate shavings

1. Coat 2 (8-inch) round cake pans with cooking spray; line pans with wax paper, and coat with cooking spray.

2. Combine brownie mix and next 3 ingredients in a large bowl; stir in pecans. Spread batter evenly into prepared pans. Bake at 350° for 25 minutes. Let cool in pans on wire racks 5 minutes; invert onto wire racks. Carefully remove wax paper, and let cake layers cool completely on wire racks.

3. Combine whipping cream and coffee granules. Beat at medium speed with an electric mixer until foamy; gradually add powdered sugar, beating until stiff peaks form. Spread whipped cream mixture between layers and on top and sides of cake. Cover and chill 1 to 2 hours. Garnish, if desired. Store in refrigerator.

Chocolate Éclair Cake

One box of graham crackers contains three individually wrapped packages of crackers; use one package for each layer of this indulgent dessert.

1 (14.4-oz.) box honey graham crackers
2 (3.4-oz.) packages French vanilla instant pudding mix
3 cups milk

1 (12-oz.) container frozen whipped topping, thawed
1 (16-oz.) container ready-to-spread chocolate frosting

1. Line bottom of an ungreased 13- x 9-inch dish with one-third of graham crackers.

2. Whisk together pudding mix and milk; add whipped topping, stirring until mixture thickens. Spread half of pudding mixture over graham crackers. Repeat layers with one-third of graham crackers and remaining pudding mixture. Top with remaining graham crackers. Spread with chocolate frosting. Cover and chill 8 hours.

If you would like to lighten this recipe, use reduced-fat graham crackers, sugar-free pudding mix, fat-free milk, and fat-free frozen whipped topping.

Chocolate Chip Cookie Cheesecake

A no-bake cheesecake, store-bought cookies, and a few extra goodies produce a winning dessert. We preferred the texture of firm chocolate chip cookies added.

1 (11.1-oz.) package no-bake cheesecake dessert (we tested with Jell-O)

⅓ cup chocolate cookie crumbs (we tested with chocolate teddy bear-shaped cookies)

½ cup butter or margarine, melted

14 chocolate chip cookies (we tested with Chips Ahoy)

¼ cup fudge sauce

1½ cups cold milk

1 (3-oz.) package cream cheese, softened

1½ cups frozen whipped topping, thawed

2 Tbsp. fudge sauce

1. Prepare crust for cheesecake according to package directions, adding chocolate cookie crumbs and melted butter. Press into a 9-inch pieplate.

2. Arrange 8 cookies in a single layer in crust; drizzle with ¼ cup fudge sauce.

3. Prepare filling according to package directions, using 1½ cups milk and beating in softened cream cheese; spoon into crust. Cover and chill 8 hours.

4. Spread whipped topping over filling. Chop remaining 6 cookies; sprinkle over whipped topping. Drizzle with 2 Tbsp. fudge sauce. Chill until ready to serve.

Chocolate-Cranberry Roulade

Unsweetened cocoa
4 large eggs
½ cup water

1 (18.25 or 18.5-oz.) package Swiss chocolate, devil's food, or fudge cake mix
Cranberry Filling

1. Coat 2 (15- x 10-inch) jelly-roll pans with cooking spray; line with parchment paper. Coat parchment paper with cooking spray, and dust with cocoa, shaking out excess. Set aside.

2. Beat eggs in a large mixing bowl at medium-high speed with an electric mixer 5 minutes. Add ½ cup water, beating at low speed just until blended. Gradually add cake mix, beating until moistened; beat at medium-high speed 2 minutes. Divide batter in half, and spread evenly into prepared pans. (Layers will be thin.)

3. Bake each cake at 350° on middle rack (in separate ovens) for 10 minutes or until cake springs back when lightly touched in center. (If you don't have a double oven, bake 1 cake at a time.)

4. Remove cakes from ovens, and immediately loosen from sides of pans. Turn out onto cloth towels dusted with cocoa. Peel off parchment paper. While cakes are warm, roll up each cake and towel together, beginning at narrow end. Place seam side down on wire racks, and let cool completely. Gently unroll cooled cakes, and spread with Cranberry Filling. Reroll cakes without towel; cover and freeze at least 1 hour.

5. Dust each cake with cocoa just before serving, and cut into 1- to 2-inch slices. Serve with remaining cranberry mixture. Garnish, if desired.

Cranberry Filling

MAKES 2 CUPS

1 (12-oz.) container cranberry-raspberry relish or cranberry-orange relish
1 cup cranberry juice cocktail

2 Tbsp. powdered sugar
1½ Tbsp. cornstarch
2 cups whipping cream

1. Process first 4 ingredients in a blender or food processor until smooth, stopping several times to scrape down sides.

2. Pour mixture into a small saucepan; bring to a boil over medium heat, stirring constantly. Boil 1 minute, stirring constantly. Remove from heat; let stand 1 hour or until completely cooled.

3. Beat whipping cream with an electric mixer until soft peaks form. Fold in ⅔ cup cranberry mixture; cover and chill remaining cranberry mixture to serve on the side or for other uses.

Caramel-Chocolate Tartlets

Dulce de leche means "sweet milk" but it tastes like caramel. It makes these bite-size sweets really rich. Make the tartlets ahead, and freeze them in the plastic pastry trays sealed in zip-top freezer bags.

1 (13.4-oz.) can dulce de leche (we tested with Nestlé)*

2 (2.1-oz.) packages frozen mini phyllo pastry shells, thawed (we tested with Athens)

1 cup double chocolate morsels (we tested with Ghirardelli) or semisweet morsels

⅓ cup roasted salted peanuts, chopped, or coarsely chopped pecans, or both

1. Spoon 1 heaping tsp. dulce de leche into each pastry shell. Microwave chocolate morsels in a microwave-safe bowl at HIGH 1 to 1½ minutes or until melted, stirring twice. Spoon 1 tsp. chocolate over dulce de leche. Sprinkle tartlets with peanuts or pecans. Freeze 1 minute to set chocolate.

*Find dulce de leche on the baking aisle by sweetened condensed milk, on the Mexican food aisle, or make your own. Pour 1 (14-oz.) can sweetened condensed milk into an 8-inch pieplate; cover with aluminum foil. Pour ½ inch hot water into a larger pan. Place covered pieplate in pan of water. Bake at 425° for 1 hour and 25 minutes or until thick and caramel colored (add hot water to pan as needed). Remove foil; cool.

Brownie Freezer Soufflés

These soufflés are great for entertaining—you can make them
ahead, and then send them from freezer to oven during dinner.

Butter
Sugar
¼ cup butter or margarine
2 (3-oz.) dark chocolate bars (we tested
   with Ghirardelli)
3 Tbsp. all-purpose flour
1 cup chocolate milk

¼ tsp. salt
1 tsp. vanilla extract
4 large eggs, separated
½ cup sugar
¼ tsp. cream of tartar
Irish Cream Sauce

1. Butter bottom and sides of 8 (6-oz.) ramekins; sprinkle with sugar. Set aside.

2. Melt ¼ cup butter and chocolate in a saucepan over medium-low heat. Add flour; stir
until smooth. Cook 1 minute, stirring constantly. Gradually add chocolate milk; cook over
medium heat, stirring constantly, until thickened and bubbly. Stir in salt and vanilla.

3. Beat egg yolks and ½ cup sugar at medium speed with an electric mixer until blended.
Gradually stir about one-fourth of hot chocolate mixture into yolk mixture; beat at medium
speed until blended. Gradually add remaining chocolate mixture, beating until blended. Let
cool 5 minutes.

4. Beat egg whites and cream of tartar at high speed until stiff peaks form. Gently fold one-
fourth of egg white into chocolate mixture. Gradually fold remaining egg white into chocolate mixture; carefully spoon into prepared ramekins. Cover and freeze until firm.

5. Remove soufflés from freezer, and let stand 30 minutes. Bake at 350° for 30 minutes or
until puffed. Cut a slit in top of each soufflé; serve immediately with Irish Cream Sauce.

Irish Cream Sauce   MAKES 1¼ CUPS

¾ cup French vanilla ice cream
3 Tbsp. Irish Cream liqueur

⅓ cup whipping cream, whipped

1. Place ice cream in a microwave-safe bowl; microwave at HIGH 30 seconds or just until
melted. Stir in Irish Cream; fold in whipped cream. Store in refrigerator.

Double-Chocolate Cookies

It takes just four ingredients and a few minutes to whip up a batch of these melt-in-your-mouth goodies.

1 (18.25-oz.) package devil's food cake mix with pudding
½ cup vegetable oil

2 large eggs
1 cup semisweet chocolate morsels

1. Combine first 3 ingredients, and beat at medium speed with an electric mixer until blended. Stir in chocolate morsels.

2. Drop dough by rounded teaspoonfuls about 2 inches apart onto ungreased baking sheets.

3. Bake at 350° for 10 minutes. Cool cookies on baking sheets 5 minutes; transfer to wire racks to cool completely.

"Other things are just food. But chocolate is chocolate."—*Patrick Skene Catling*

Roasted-Pecan Clusters

This recipe is so simple, yet so yummy. Toasting the pecans really brings out their flavor and crunch.

3 Tbsp. butter or margarine
3 cups pecan pieces

6 (2-oz.) squares chocolate candy coating

1. Melt butter in a 15- x 10-inch jelly-roll pan in a 300° oven. Spread nuts in pan.

2. Bake at 300° for 30 minutes, stirring every 10 minutes.

3. Microwave candy coating in a microwave-safe bowl at MEDIUM (50% power) 2 to 3 minutes or until melted. Stir in nuts. Drop by rounded teaspoonfuls onto wax paper; let cool. Peel from wax paper, and store in an airtight container.

Using a shallow pan ensures the pecans roast properly. You can roast the pecans ahead, cool completely, and store in an airtight container.

Banana-Split Brownies

Stir a palmful of sweet ingredients into a brownie mix to create this sensational treat.

1 (17.6-ounce) package chocolate double-fudge brownie mix (we tested with Duncan Hines Chocolate Lover's Double Fudge Brownie Mix)
½ cup dried cherries
¼ cup water
1 medium banana, sliced
1 teaspoon vanilla extract

½ cup sliced almonds, toasted (optional)
Toppings: ice cream, hot fudge and caramel sauces, toasted flaked coconut, grated milk chocolate, chopped pecans, candy-coated chocolate pieces, whipping cream, maraschino cherries with stems

1. Prepare brownie mix according to package directions, following cakelike instructions.

2. Microwave cherries and ¼ cup water at HIGH 1½ minutes. Drain and cool.

3. Stir cherries, banana, vanilla, and, if desired, almonds into batter.

4. Pour into a lightly greased 8- x 8-inch baking pan.

5. Bake at 350° for 40 to 45 minutes. Cool and cut brownies into squares. Serve with desired toppings.

To remove brownies easily from the pan, line the pan with aluminum foil. Allow enough foil to hang over the edges so you can use it as handles.

Chocolate Crescents

A three-ingredient chocolate treat—life is good!

1 (8-oz.) package refrigerated crescent
   dinner rolls

24 milk chocolate kisses
   Powdered sugar

1. Unroll refrigerated crescent dinner rolls, and separate each dough portion along center and diagonal perforations, forming 8 triangles.

2. Place 2 chocolate kisses, points up, on wide end of each triangle; place a third chocolate between the 2 chocolates, point down. Starting at wide end of triangle, roll dough over chocolates, pinching edges to seal. Place rolls, sealed sides down, on an ungreased baking sheet. Shape into crescents.

3. Bake at 375° for 10 minutes or until lightly browned. Cool crescents slightly, and sprinkle with powdered sugar. Serve warm.

"Money talks. Chocolate sings."

—Unknown

Chocolate for Giving

"The 12-step chocoholics program: Never be more than 12 steps away from chocolate."

—*Terry Moore*

Chocolate-Caramel-Nut Surprise Cake

If you'd like to share this decadent cake, bake it in a disposable pan, cover and wrap with ribbon, and deliver to a friend along with a jar of caramel sauce for extra indulgence. Gift giving doesn't get any easier.

1 (18.25-oz.) package German chocolate cake mix with pudding (we tested with Pillsbury)
1 (14-oz.) package caramels
½ cup butter or margarine
⅓ cup milk
1 cup chopped dry-roasted peanuts
¾ cup milk chocolate morsels
Caramel sauce (optional)

1. Prepare cake mix according to package directions. Pour half of batter into a greased and floured 13- x 9-inch pan. Bake at 350° for 10 minutes. (Cake will not test done.) Cool cake in pan on a wire rack 10 minutes.

2. Meanwhile, unwrap caramels. Combine caramels, butter, and milk in a heavy saucepan, and cook over medium heat until caramels melt, stirring often. Spread over cake.

3. Sprinkle peanuts and chocolate morsels over caramel mixture. Spread remaining cake batter evenly over top. Bake at 350° for 25 to 30 more minutes. Cool in pan on wire rack. Cut into squares. Drizzle with caramel sauce, if desired.

Triple-Chocolate Coffee Cakes

Drizzle this rich chocolate snack cake first with white chocolate and then with semisweet chocolate for extra indulgence before topping with pecans. This recipe makes two cakes, so give one to a friend and savor the other yourself.

1 (18.25-oz.) package devil's food cake mix
1 (3.9-oz.) package chocolate instant pudding mix
2 cups sour cream
1 cup butter or margarine, softened
5 large eggs
1 tsp. vanilla extract
3 cups semisweet chocolate morsels, divided
1 cup white chocolate morsels
1 cup chopped pecans, toasted

1. Beat first 6 ingredients at low speed with an electric mixer 30 seconds or just until moistened; beat at medium speed 2 minutes. Stir in 2 cups semisweet chocolate morsels; pour batter evenly into 2 greased and floured 9-inch square cake pans.

2. Bake at 350° for 25 to 30 minutes or until a wooden pick inserted in center comes out clean. Cool completely in pans on wire racks.

3. Microwave white chocolate morsels in a glass bowl at HIGH 30 to 60 seconds or until morsels melt, stirring at 30-second intervals until smooth. Drizzle evenly over cakes; repeat procedure with remaining cup of semisweet morsels. Sprinkle cakes evenly with pecans.

Make these cakes a couple of weeks ahead. Once cooled, cover tightly in foil; place in a zip-top plastic bag and freeze. Thaw at room temperature.

Chocolate-Raspberry Petits Fours

Place these moist little brownie bites in candy cups for gift giving, if you'd like. They're very pretty, and no one will know you started with prebaked brownies.

2 (11-oz.) boxes prebaked mini brownies (we tested with Entenmann's Little Bites Brownies)

⅓ cup seedless raspberry jam

1 Tbsp. raspberry liqueur (optional)

1 (15-oz.) container pourable milk chocolate frosting (we tested with Betty Crocker)

½ cup white chocolate morsels

1. Place brownies on a wire rack set over a baking sheet.

2. Microwave jam in a glass measuring cup at HIGH 10 to 15 seconds or just until slightly melted; stir until smooth. Stir in liqueur, if desired. Pour a small amount of jam into a flavor injector; inject each brownie through the side with a small amount of jam. Refill injector as needed until all brownies are filled.

3. Microwave pourable frosting in original container at HIGH 20 seconds. Pour or spoon frosting over brownies. If additional frosting is needed, scrape off excess frosting from baking sheet, and reheat.

4. Microwave white chocolate morsels in a glass measuring cup on HIGH 1 minute or until melted, stirring after 30 seconds. Place white chocolate in a zip-top freezer bag. Snip a tiny hole in 1 corner of bag; drizzle melted white chocolate over brownies. Chill brownies 30 minutes or until chocolate is firm.

Look for plastic flavor injectors in the kitchen gadget section at houseware stores or supermarkets.

Double-Chip Oatmeal Cookies

Chocolate and peanut butter chips take oatmeal cookies to new levels.

¾ cup butter or margarine, softened
¼ cup shortening
¾ cup granulated sugar
¾ cup firmly packed light brown sugar
2 large eggs
1 tsp. vanilla extract
2¼ cups all-purpose flour
1 tsp. baking soda

¼ tsp. salt
1 (11-oz. package) peanut butter and milk chocolate morsels
1 (12-oz.) package semisweet chocolate morsels
½ cup uncooked regular oats
½ cup chopped pecans, toasted

1. Beat butter and shortening at medium speed with an electric mixer until creamy; gradually add sugars, beating until blended. Add eggs and vanilla, beating until blended.

2. Combine flour, soda, and salt; gradually add to butter mixture, beating well. Stir in morsels, oats, and pecans.

3. Drop dough by ¼ cupfuls onto lightly greased baking sheets. Bake at 350° for 15 to 16 minutes or until golden around edges. Remove to wire racks to cool.

Mocha-Chocolate Shortbread

Chocolate morsels quickly melt when sprinkled over the warm shortbread; spread them into a quick glaze.

1 ¼ cups all-purpose flour
½ cup powdered sugar
2 tsp. instant coffee granules
⅔ cup butter or margarine, softened

½ tsp. vanilla extract
1 (12-oz.) package semisweet chocolate morsels, divided
Vanilla or coffee ice cream (optional)

1. Combine first 3 ingredients in a medium bowl; add butter and vanilla, and beat at low speed with an electric mixer until blended. Stir in 1 cup chocolate morsels.

2. Press dough into an ungreased 9-inch square pan; prick dough with a fork.

3. Bake at 325° for 20 minutes or until lightly browned. Sprinkle remaining 1 cup morsels over top, and spread to cover. Cut shortbread into 25 (about 1¾-inch) squares; cut each square into 2 triangles. Let cool 30 minutes in pan before removing. Serve with ice cream, if desired.

"Nine out of 10 people like chocolate.
The tenth person always lies." —*John Q. Tullius*

No-Bake Peanut Butter Cookies

You can stir these chocolate, peanut butter, and oat cookies together in no time. Make them regular size or drop them from ¼ cup measures to make jumbo treats.

2 cups sugar
¼ cup cocoa
½ cup butter or margarine
½ cup milk

½ tsp. vanilla extract
½ cup creamy or chunky peanut butter
3 cups uncooked quick-cooking oats

1. Combine first 5 ingredients in a medium saucepan. Cook over low heat until butter melts, stirring occasionally. Increase heat to medium; bring to a boil. Boil 1 minute. Remove from heat; quickly stir in peanut butter until smooth. Stir in oats. Quickly drop by heaping table-spoonfuls onto wax paper. Let cool completely. Carefully remove from wax paper. Store in an airtight container.

Jumbo Cookies

Quickly drop cookie dough by ¼ cupfuls onto wax paper.

Peanut Butter Cup Cookies

Nestle peanut butter cup candies in the center of warm cookies for a quick treat not soon forgotten.

1	cup butter, softened	1	Tbsp. fresh lemon juice
1	cup powdered sugar	5¼	cups all-purpose flour
1	cup granulated sugar	1	tsp. cream of tartar
2	large eggs	1	tsp. baking soda
1	cup vegetable oil	¼	tsp. salt
2	tsp. vanilla extract	84	miniature peanut butter cups

1. Beat butter at medium speed with an electric mixer until fluffy; add powdered and granulated sugars, beating well. Add eggs, oil, vanilla, and lemon juice, beating until blended.

2. Combine flour and next 3 ingredients; gradually add to sugar mixture, beating until blended.

3. Shape dough into 1-inch balls, and place about 2 inches apart on lightly greased baking sheets.

4. Bake in batches at 350° for 9 to 11 minutes or until set. (Do not brown.) Immediately place a miniature peanut butter cup in the center of each cookie. Remove to wire racks to cool.

Chocolate-Covered Cherry Cookies

Hand-dipped cherries crown each cookie and a cherry liqueur-laced glaze is drizzled over the top.

⅓ cup butter, softened
⅓ cup shortening
1 large egg
1 (17.5-oz.) package chocolate chip cookie mix (we tested with Betty Crocker)
½ cup unsweetened cocoa

42 assorted chocolate-covered cherries (we tested with Russell Stover hand-dipped cherry cordials)
½ cup powdered sugar
4 to 5 tsp. cherry liqueur or maraschino cherry juice

1. Beat butter and shortening in a large bowl at medium speed with an electric mixer until fluffy; add egg, beating until blended.

2. Combine cookie mix and cocoa; gradually add to butter mixture, beating well. Shape dough into 1-inch balls. Place balls 2 inches apart on ungreased baking sheets.

3. Bake at 375° for 8 to 10 minutes. Cool 2 minutes. Gently press 1 cherry candy in center of each cookie. Cool completely on baking sheets; transfer to wire racks.

4. Combine powdered sugar and liqueur in a small bowl, stirring until smooth. (Glaze should be thick, yet easy to drizzle.) Place glaze in a small zip-top plastic bag. Snip a tiny hole in 1 corner of bag. Drizzle glaze over cookies. Let stand until set.

Chocolate Fudge Brownies

This basic brownie recipe is one of our favorites and offers lots of options. If you're a fan of nuts, stir 1 cup chopped, toasted pecans into the batter.

4 (1-oz.) unsweetened chocolate baking squares
1 cup butter, softened
2 cups granulated sugar
4 large eggs

1 cup all-purpose flour
1 tsp. vanilla extract
1 cup semisweet chocolate morsels
Powdered sugar (optional)

1. Microwave chocolate squares in a small microwave-safe bowl at MEDIUM (50% power) 1½ minutes, stirring at 30-second intervals, until melted. Stir until smooth.

2. Beat butter and granulated sugar at medium speed with an electric mixer until light and fluffy. Add eggs, 1 at a time, beating just until blended after each addition. Add melted chocolate, beating just until blended.

3. Add flour, beating at low speed just until blended. Stir in vanilla and chocolate morsels. Spread batter into a greased and floured 13- x 9-inch pan.

4. Bake at 350° for 35 to 40 minutes or until center is set. Cool completely on a wire rack. Sift powdered sugar over tops, if desired. Cut into squares.

Praline-Pecan Brownies

Prepare and bake Chocolate Fudge Brownies as directed; cool completely. Spread uncut brownies evenly with Chocolate Glaze (recipe on page 26); sprinkle evenly with 2 cups coarsely chopped pecans.

Caramel-Coconut-Pecan Brownies

Prepare batter for Chocolate Fudge Brownies as directed; spread batter into a greased and floured 13- x 9-inch pan. Sprinkle batter evenly with 2 cups sweetened flaked coconut, 1 (12-oz.) package semisweet chocolate morsels, and 1½ cups chopped pecans. Drizzle evenly with 1 (14-oz.) can sweetened condensed milk. Bake at 350° for 50 to 55 minutes or until golden brown and set.

Congo Bars

Everyone likes an easy bar cookie recipe that gets rave reviews.
This is one of them.

2 cups firmly packed brown sugar
½ cup butter or margarine, melted
3 large eggs, lightly beaten
1 tsp. vanilla extract
1½ cups all-purpose flour
1 cup graham cracker crumbs (about
6 whole crackers)

2 tsp. baking powder
1 cup salted cashews, chopped
1 (11.5-oz.) package semisweet
chocolate chunks

1. Stir together first 4 ingredients. Combine flour, graham cracker crumbs, and baking powder; add to butter mixture, stirring well. Stir in cashews and chocolate chunks. (Batter will be thick.) Spread batter into a greased 13- x 9-inch pan; press gently into pan.

2. Bake at 350° for 27 to 30 minutes. Cool completely in pan on a wire rack. Cut into bars.

"There's nothing better than a good friend, except a good friend with chocolate."

—*Linda Grayson,* The Pickwick Papers

Crispy Chocolate Hearts

These heart-shaped treats make great Valentine's gifts. Use an egg-shaped cookie cutter for Easter and a tree-shaped cookie cutter for Christmas.

1 (12-oz.) package semisweet chocolate morsels*
½ cup creamy peanut butter
2 cups crisp rice cereal
1½ cups peanuts

1½ cups miniature marshmallows
2 (2-oz.) chocolate candy coating squares, melted
White nonpareils (optional)

1. Microwave chocolate morsels in a large glass bowl at HIGH 2 minutes or until melted, stirring chocolate every 30 seconds.

2. Stir in peanut butter, stirring until well blended.

3. Stir in cereal, peanuts, and marshmallows. Line a 13- x 9-inch pan with aluminum foil. Lightly grease foil. Press mixture into foil-lined pan. Drizzle with chocolate. Sprinkle with white nonpareils, if desired.

4. Let stand 1 hour or until firm; cut with a 3-inch heart-shaped cookie cutter to make hearts. Store in an airtight container or place in a candy box, if desired.

*Substitute 6 (2-oz.) almond bark candy coating squares for chocolate morsels, if desired.

White Chocolate Party Mix

We couldn't keep our hands off this crunchy sweet-and-salty snack.

1 (14-oz.) package candy-coated chocolate-covered peanuts

1 (9-oz.) package butter-flavored pretzels (we tested with Snyder's of Hanover Butter Snaps Pretzels)

5 cups toasted oat O-shaped cereal (we tested with Cheerios)

5 cups crispy corn cereal snack mix (we tested with Corn Chex snack mix)

1 (24-oz.) package almond bark candy coating

1. Combine first 4 ingredients in a large container; set aside.

2. Microwave candy coating in a microwave-safe dish at HIGH 1 minute, stirring once. Microwave at HIGH for 1 more minute; stir until smooth. Pour over cereal mixture, stirring to combine. Spread on wax paper, and let cool 30 minutes.

3. Break apart, and store in an airtight container.

"Caramels are only a fad. Chocolate is a permanent thing."—*Milton Snavely Hershey*

Chocolate Cordial Cherries

Brandy-soaked cherries can be left in the freezer for up to
two days before dipping them in chocolate. The longer you
freeze them the more brandy flavor they take on.

1 (10-oz.) jar maraschino cherries with
   stems
½ cup brandy (optional)

1 (8-oz.) package semisweet chocolate
   baking squares, chopped

1. Drain cherries, and return cherries to jar. Pour brandy, if desired, into jar; cover with lid,
and freeze 8 hours. Drain cherries, reserving brandy for another use; pat cherries dry.

2. Melt two-thirds of chocolate baking squares in a saucepan over medium heat, stirring until
a candy thermometer reaches 115°. Remove from heat; add remaining chocolate, and stir
until candy thermometer reaches 89° and chocolate is smooth.

3. Dip cherries quickly into melted chocolate, coating well. Place cherries on wax paper,
stem sides up, and cool.

Strawberry Fudge Balls

Roll some of these fudgy nuggets in each of the three coating options to vary their look.

1 (8-oz.) package cream cheese, softened
1 cup (6 oz.) semisweet chocolate morsels, melted
¾ cup vanilla wafer crumbs

¼ cup strawberry preserves
Coatings: 1 cup almonds, toasted and finely chopped; powdered sugar; unsweetened cocoa

1. Beat cream cheese at medium speed with an electric mixer until fluffy. Add melted chocolate, beating until smooth. Stir in wafer crumbs and preserves; cover and chill 1 hour.

2. Shape mixture into 1-inch balls, and roll in almonds, powdered sugar, or cocoa. Store in an airtight container in refrigerator up to 1 week, or freeze up to 1 month.

Five Pounds of Chocolate Fudge

Slice small squares of this creamy fudge for serving or cut large slabs for gift giving.

2 (12-oz.) packages semisweet
   chocolate morsels
1 cup butter or margarine
1 (7-oz.) jar marshmallow cream
4½ cups sugar

1 (12-oz.) can evaporated milk
2 Tbsp. vanilla extract
1½ cups chopped pecans, toasted
   Butter or margarine

1. Combine first 3 ingredients in a large mixing bowl; set aside.

2. Combine sugar and evaporated milk in a buttered Dutch oven.

3. Cook sugar mixture over medium heat, stirring occasionally, until mixture reaches soft ball stage or a candy thermometer registers 234°; pour over chocolate mixture. Beat at high speed with an electric mixer or with a wooden spoon until mixture thickens and begins to lose its gloss. Stir in vanilla and chopped pecans.

4. Spread into a buttered 15- x 10-inch jelly-roll pan. Cover and chill until firm. Cut into 1-inch squares. Store in an airtight container at room temperature.

Check your candy thermometer for accuracy. When placed in a pan of boiling water, the thermometer should register 212°.

Texas Millionaires

Store these in the refrigerator rather than the freezer because
freezer temperatures can change the color of the chocolate.

1 (14-oz.) package caramels
2 Tbsp. butter or margarine
2 Tbsp. water

3 cups pecan halves
1 cup semisweet chocolate morsels
8 (2-oz.) vanilla candy coating squares

1. Cook first 3 ingredients in a heavy saucepan over low heat, stirring constantly until
smooth. Stir in pecan halves. Cool in pan 5 minutes.

2. Drop by tablespoonfuls onto lightly greased wax paper. Chill 1 hour, or freeze 20 minutes
or until firm.

3. Melt morsels and candy coating in a heavy saucepan over low heat, stirring until smooth.
Dip caramel candies into chocolate mixture, allowing excess to drip; place on lightly greased
wax paper. Let stand until firm.

Cocoa Mix

This mix makes a gracious plenty for several gifts—with some left over for your family.

3 (9.6-oz.) packages instant nonfat dry milk powder (11½ cups)
1 (16-oz.) package powdered sugar, sifted

2 (8-oz.) cans unsweetened cocoa
1 (6-oz.) jar powdered nondairy coffee creamer

1. Combine all ingredients; stir well. Store in an airtight container. Use according to gift card directions below.

Directions for gift card: Place ¼ cup cocoa mix in a mug; add boiling water, and stir to dissolve. Top with marshmallows, if desired.

Index